P9-CPW-126

Dec 2010

THE 25 MOST COMMON SALES MISTAKES AND HOW TO AVOID THEM

3RD EDITION

STEPHAN SCHIFFMAN

AMERICA'S #1 CORPORATE SALES TRAINER

A
BUSINESS

Avon, Massachusetts

To your future

• • •

Published by
Adams Business, an imprint of Adams Media,
a division of F+W Media, Inc.
57 Littlefield Street, Avon, MA 02322. U.S.A.
www.adamsmedia.com

ISBN 10: 1-59869-821-4
ISBN 13: 978-1-59869-821-3

Printed in the United States of America.

J I H G F E D C B

Library of Congress Cataloging-in-Publication Data
is available from the publisher.

This publication is designed to provide accurate and authoritative information with regard to the subject matter covered. It is sold with the understanding that the publisher is not engaged in rendering legal, accounting, or other professional advice. If legal advice or other expert assistance is required, the services of a competent professional person should be sought.

—From a *Declaration of Principles* jointly adopted by a Committee of the American Bar Association and a Committee of Publishers and Associations

Many of the designations used by manufacturers and sellers to distinguish their product are claimed as trademarks. Where those designations appear in this book and Adams Media was aware of a trademark claim, the designations have been printed with initial capital letters.

*This book is available at quantity discounts for bulk purchases.
For information, please call 1-800-289-0963.*

Contents

Bonus Mistakes

Acknowledgments

I would like to thank the following people for their help with this book: Anne, Daniele, and Jennifer for their unceasing support.

Introduction to the Third Edition

Once or twice a year I'm asked to revise one of my old books. Some might suspect that revisiting old work is boring in a déjà vu, been-there-done-that kind of way. On the contrary, I look forward to it.

For one thing, looking back reaffirms the basic tenets of my sales philosophy. I make very few changes of any kind and none of any substantive nature. If these books required substantial revision, it would mean that what I've been preaching is wrong.

But sometimes there are amusing aspects to my nostalgic trips back in time. For example, somewhere in the middle of a prior edition of this book I suggested it is appropriate to send a thank-you note to a prospect following a first visit, a reminder of what was discussed and that you'll be getting back to him shortly. Moreover, I even told you how to prepare the note on a "good typewriter."

Can you even find a good typewriter in an office now?

Technological advances aside, the basic "to don't" list offered here is as valid today as it was when it was first written about a decade and a half ago.

In fact, the rules may be more pertinent today than they were then. As this introduction is being written, the American economy is in terrible shape. Oil prices, which were outrageously high, are lower—but who knows for how long. We're in the midst of a mortgage crisis. And unemployment is the highest it's been in years. There's even talk that America's largest auto companies are being driven to bankruptcy.

Hopefully, all that will have changed by the time you read these words. With any degree of luck, we'll all be back on the road to prosperity. But in an ironic way, I believe these down times are good for us.

When we—and by "we" I mean sales reps—go through a period of prosperity, we tend to get sloppy. Orders come in so easily—whether we do things correctly or not—that we forget the basics. Bad times serve as a wake-up call, a reminder that if we continue to make silly (okay, stupid) errors, someone else will get the business.

The original version of this book included twenty-five common sales mistakes—and how to avoid them. I've added five new "mistakes"—reflecting patterns of errors I've noticed in classes over the last few years.

Finally, I've always been a little leery of part of this book's title: *25 Most Common Sales Mistakes* blaring across the cover struck me as a little negative. I always suspected that that was all potential readers ever saw. People never like to be told that they're doing something incorrectly. I understand that. That's why I think it's important to focus on the other part of the title—how to avoid them, how to stay on track, how to close sales in any environment.

I think you'll enjoy this book. More important, I think you'll profit from it. And if you have any suggestions, feel free to contact me in care of *sschiffman@steveschiffman.com*.

I answer all correspondence. Especially the letters from people who enjoyed the book.

Stephan Schiffman
February 2009
New York City

Introduction

This book is not a cure-all; it doesn't promise an instant turnaround to your sales career. My feeling is that, without your efforts and commitment to your own results, no book can do that.

This book can, however, be used as an effective tool for identifying and resolving the most common and troublesome sales mistakes—the ones that needlessly eat away at commission dollars. If that's a topic of concern to you, read on.

If you've ever watched the summer Olympic swimming competitions, you've no doubt noticed that the winners of these races tend to win by very slim margins—tenths or hundredths of a second. That's remarkable, isn't it? That when the top athletes in the field come together, the amount of time separating them at the finish line is often about as much time as it takes to snap your fingers?

I think sales is sometimes very similar. The competition out there can be brutal; victories are often decided by hairbreadth margins. Lose three or four important hairbreadth races in a row, and you're out of business; win three or four, and you're tops in your field.

That's where this book comes in. The solutions I've offered to the most common sales mistakes are designed to help you add to your personal sales efficiency—a little bit here, a little bit there. I'm not out to reinvent the wheel with this book, but rather to give you enough of an edge in enough common problem areas to make victory more likely for you in a tough race. The book is designed to be read easily and quickly. You won't find long discourses on psychology or personal interaction here, but rather tangible ideas you can put into practice immediately.

My favorite kind of sales book is one you can read in a day or two and get impressive results from immediately. I believe this is that kind of book, and I think you will too.

Let me know if you agree. Write to me about this book and how it works for you. Here's my address:

Stephan Schiffman
c/o Adams Media/Publishers
57 Littlefield Street
Avon, MA 02322 USA

Good luck!

Not Being Obsessed

You must like what you are doing for a living—selling— enough to become obsessed with it. Not fifteen-hours-a- day obsessed, but rather I-have-absolutely-got-to-do-this- right-day-in-and-day-out obsessed.

For my money, the most crucial word in sales today is obsession; close behind it are two supporting ideas, utiliza- tion and implementation. Let's talk a little bit about what these three words really mean for you.

Obsession

Every day, I make twenty cold calls. And by making twenty cold calls, I can get through to maybe seven peo- ple. Once I get through to seven people, I'll usually set up one appointment. I do that five days a week, which, by extension, means that every week, I have, on average, five new sales appointments. I close one out of five, so at the end of the year, I should have fifty new customers.

I mention my daily routine—my obsession, if you will, my repetitive, second-nature approach to sales—so that you'll know I'm not just talking theory here. Many sales books are written by people who have retired or gotten out of business. I have not retired, I'm too young to retire, and I'm having too much fun to get out of business. I am an active, professional salesperson. I also happen to be president of one of the country's top sales training firms; part of the reason for our success is that the people we work with know that we practice exactly what we preach, day in and day out.

In order for you to be successful in sales, you must be absolutely, positively obsessed with your work while you're doing it. You have to be so dedicated to the idea that you can satisfy a customer with your product or service that you move into a whole new work realm: a realm where there is simply no place for watching the clock, wishing it were time for a coffee break, or wondering how the Jets are going to do against the Patriots Sunday. That's not to say there's no place for any of these things in your life—just that there's no place for any of these things while you're working. Now, this doesn't mean you must take yourself so seriously that you become a workaholic and have a heart attack at thirty-eight. It means you must make a commitment to yourself, and build up a routine that is success oriented.

Of course, we should note here that obsession without discipline often results in chaos. As obsessive as you want to get about being successful, all that energy must be coupled with discipline or you're not going to get anywhere.

Utilization
This means utilizing everything at your disposal to increase your success. In a way, it's being obsessive about getting the most from your environment.

Burrow through company brochures and catalogs to learn everything you can about your product. Have regular meetings with your sales manager to discuss your performance and get new ideas. Use books like this one, or motivational tapes, to put you on the right track. In short, utilize your tools! Such tools needn't be limited to things you can hold in your hand. Have you shown customers your office or plant? Have you reviewed past company successes with your prospect? Have you invited current and potential clients to company social outings? Be creative. Once you stop to think about it, you'll be amazed at how many excellent tools go completely ignored by salespeople.

Implementation

Or, if you prefer, just do it; make the effort in the first place. All the sales books in the world won't help you if you don't try.

Don't fall prey to the "paralysis of analysis." One of the beautiful things about sales is that it's an extremely binary way to make a living. You're either making a sale or you're not. Make every effort to be "on" during every moment you actually communicate with potential customers. Take nothing for granted, and don't get bogged down with overpreparation. Do it.

I realize, of course, that research has its place. But you should never forget that if you don't make the calls, your efforts are going to be in vain. Selling is selling: going after people and talking to them. Don't lose sight of that, and don't let your obsession be misdirected into something that won't help you put numbers on the board.

Three crucial ideas—obsession, implementation, and utilization. How do you make sure you're incorporating them? Here are some tips:

Make a to-do list. Identify important objectives before you start the day; then work like crazy to attain the objectives on your list.

Keep your motivation up. This book is an excellent start; you might also eventually turn to motivational tapes or seminars. Whatever your approach, make a commitment to find one new idea a month and run with it.

Start early. Try coming into the office forty-five minutes before everyone else does. You'll be amazed at what you can accomplish, and how big a jump you'll get on your day. Don't think of it as an inconvenience—think of it as an advantage. And just do it.

Be obsessive, but disciplined. Utilize everything you have at your fingertips; then implement. It's a proven recipe for success.

Not Listening to the Prospect

Perhaps the easiest way to distinguish successful salespeople from unsuccessful ones is to watch how they interact with a prospect. Do they do all the talking, never letting the prospect get a word in edgewise? If so, it's a good bet you're looking at a failure.

You must let the prospect speak about himself or herself; the information you'll receive as a result is invaluable. Ramrodding your points through, and merely overpowering the person rather than showing how you can help, is a sure way for you to descend into the stereotypical "hard sell" that no one likes. Such behavior is a great way to lose sales.

To be sure, you and I really believe that our product will help the person we are sitting across the table from. And yet, even though we believe that in our bones, we have to listen—not lecture. Listening is the only way to target the product to the unique set of problems and concerns the prospect presents to us. By staying focused on the objective of helping the prospect (rather than "getting" the prospect), we build trust. And trust is vitally important.

When you get right down to it, a good salesperson doesn't so much sell as help. You can pass along important information, and ask for the sale after you've demonstrated clearly how your product can help achieve an important objective—but ultimately, the prospect has to make the decision, not you. Ideally, you have to know what it will take for the prospect to do the selling himself or herself. In this environment, listening becomes very important.

Listening doesn't just mean paying attention to the words that come out of the prospect's mouth. Very little of what we actually communicate is verbal; most is nonverbal. Be sure you're "listening" in such a way that allows you every opportunity to pick up on nonverbal cues. By doing this—letting the prospect get across what's important to him or her—you'll stand out from the vast majority of other salespeople, who simply talk too much.

When your prospect wonders something aloud, give the person enough time to complete the thought. When your prospect asks you a pointed question, do your best to answer succinctly—then listen for the reaction. Allow the speaker to complete sentences—never interrupt. (What's more, you should let the prospect interrupt you at any time to get more information from you.) Express genuine interest in the things the prospect says. Keep an ear out for subtle messages and hints the prospect may be sending you.

When you do talk or make a presentation, don't drone on; keep an eye on your prospect to make sure what you're saying is interesting. If it isn't, change gears and start asking questions about the problems the prospect faces—you are probably missing something important. Of course, you should never come across as hostile or combative to the prospect.

You probably already know that the first ten or fifteen seconds you spend with a prospect have a major impact on the way the rest of the meeting goes. This is because there is an intangible, feeling-oriented "sizing-up" phenomenon that occurs early on in any new relationship.

Much of who you are and how you are perceived as a communicator—brash or retiring, open or constricted, helpful or manipulative—will be on display in a subtle but crucial manner in the opening moments of your first meeting with someone. Make sure you are sending the messages you want to send. Before the meeting, avoid pre-occupations with subjects that have nothing to do with the client; these will carry over even if they never come up in conversation.

How do you improve your listening skills? Here's one idea. Always take notes during your meetings with prospects. As we'll see later, this dramatizes your attention and respect for the prospect's needs. (And if you think it's impossible to listen and take notes at the same time, you're wrong—the two actually reinforce each other.)

Once the conversation has begun to pick up some steam, take out a legal pad and write down the most important points the prospect makes during your presentation; read essential details back to him or her before the meeting ends. Where appropriate, ask the prospect to expand on key concerns.

7

That's all very well in theory, you may be thinking. But what if the conversation is going nowhere? How do I listen if there's nothing to listen to? Shouldn't I make a pitch?

Probably not. The odds are that, early on in the meeting, you simply do not know enough about your prospect yet to go into a long presentation. So avoid doing that. Instead, focus your questions on three simple areas: the past, the present, and the future.

What kind of widget service was used in the past? What are the company's present widget needs? What does the prospect anticipate doing with regard to widgets in the future?

Add a "how" and a "why" where appropriate, and that's really all you need. Take notes on the responses you get.

After you resummarize the points the prospect has made, you may be ready to talk in more detail about exactly what you can do to help solve the prospect's problems. But be sure that you listen first.

MISTAKE #3

Not Empathizing with the Prospect

Put yourself in the prospect's shoes—you'll understand how to sell to the person better.

An empathizing attitude is a far cry from what most salespeople feel about their customers. The typical comment I hear on the matter goes something like this: "Frankly, it doesn't matter to me why the guy bought what he bought; he bought it. And I got the commission." Does that sound to you like the way to build repeat sales?

Certainly, it is crucial to put numbers up on the board. But that's exactly why you must always make sure you're making every effort to see things from the prospect's point of view.

Sometimes salespeople forget to take into consideration what is going on in the other person's head. But think about your own experiences. Did you ever walk into a room where a person was angry, but you didn't know it? Maybe you wanted a coworker to give you a hand on a project you were having trouble with. So you stepped in and made your request in an offhand way, and before you knew it, the other person was barking out orders, stomping around the room, and generally making your life difficult.

You probably could have gotten further with your task if you'd taken a moment to size up how the other person was feeling—and why.

Try to establish what is going on in the prospect's life on a given day: what feelings are likely to surface? For example, if you are dealing with someone whose company is going through a merger, you can make a guess that the prospect may well be concerned about losing his or her job. Perhaps this is not the person who should be subjected to your most aggressive approach. Perhaps things should go a little more slowly.

Just as important, bear in mind that the prospect you are talking to is going to be doing something that many businesspeople try to avoid: talking to a salesperson. It's a little naive to assume that your first visit with someone is going to be eagerly anticipated; in all likelihood, the person has probably managed to set aside a few minutes for you out of a very busy day. Treat the prospect with respect, and realize that you are probably not the most important thing that's going to happen to him or her that day.

How do you find out about the person you are talking to, so you can empathize? The best way, of course, is to ask appropriate questions and carefully monitor what comes back to you in response. More importantly, make an effort to be sincere. Sincerity is often the last thing people expect from a salesperson.

Do you really care about the people that you talk to? If you don't, this attitude will show through. One salesperson I worked with some years ago simply could not sell to anyone younger than about forty-five. The reason?

Deep down, he really didn't respect his younger prospects. They picked up on that—even though the meetings were always cordial—and his sales suffered as a result.

Exhibit genuine concern about the person and his or her problems, and ask questions that demonstrate your care. React properly to those questions. Above all, keep your conversations straightforward and sincere—avoid peppering the person with probing questions right off the bat, and don't let your interest sound fake or forced.

This may be difficult at first. Maybe you have been bruised one time too many, or become a little jaded in your sales career. Maybe you have forgotten the fun of the business, lost sight of the thrill of making a sale as a result of a good, solid, honest initial contact. If so, you must make every effort to relearn the enthusiasm and sincerity that builds trust. That effort will pay off hand-somely for you.

MISTAKE #4

Seeing the Prospect as an Adversary

They have a saying in the advertising world: "The customer is not stupid; the customer is your spouse." I suppose you could adjust it somewhat for sales: "The prospect is not an enemy; the prospect is your fiancé."

The prospect should be your friend; always strive to get the two of you working together.

I'd like to have a dollar for every time a salesperson has talked to me about that so-and-so down the street who just welched on a deal. Or for every time I heard about someone coming on so strong that the prospect slammed down the phone receiver, or—worse still—threw the salesperson out of the office during a scheduled meeting.

I've never had a prospect of mine become an adversary, and you shouldn't either. There's simply no excuse for letting your sales work result in a large number of enemies, rather than a long list of allies.

Don't fall prey to the ridiculous advice you may hear about how you have to beat up on a prospect before he or she beats up on you. This approach is rude, arrogant, antisocial, and unprofessional. But those aren't the most important reasons not to follow that advice. You shouldn't

13

beat up on the prospect for one simple reason: doing so loses sales.

The prospect would rather be your friend. Just as you want to have the prospect like you and give you business, the prospect really would prefer to be your friend. Many salespeople find this hard to believe, but it's true. Most of the situations in which the prospect seems to cut things short have to do with either a hectic work environment or an unprofessional approach by the salesperson.

The degree to which the potential for goodwill is retained is based on how well you do your job. See your prospect as someone you want to do business with; an associate, someone you can talk to while you both work to attain goals.

The best selling arises from win-win situations. That means you win because the prospect wins. You are not out to "get the order now" if doing so is not going to help your prospect. When the prospect buys something from you, he or she is buying a benefit. That benefit (faster production, lower operating costs, higher sales, whatever) is what you must keep your eye on. Not your sales totals.

If you see your prospect as an adversary, someone you are going to outwit, outsmart, or show up, you are never going to be successful. You are, instead, going to lose that potential customer, and probably build up a bad reputation in the process.

Let me tell you a story that illustrates what I mean. Karen was a sales rep who had just started out with a major business machine company with an office in Manhattan. Karen did not yet understand that she wouldn't get anywhere by treating the prospect as an adversary. This led to some major errors in strategy on one sales call in particular. How major? Read on.

Karen had scheduled an appointment with an important prospect, one she'd been phoning for weeks. She showed up at the scheduled time, only to hear at the reception desk that her contact had had to deal with some unexpected problems, and would need to reschedule.

There are any number of ways to deal with that situation. What Karen did, however, is a textbook example of how not to deal with it.

Karen made such a fuss at the front desk that her contact actually had to drop what he was doing and make his way out to the reception area to try to explain what had happened. The contact asked politely if Karen could call tomorrow to set up another appointment. Karen refused. She'd waited long enough, she said. She had to meet with the contact now, today. After about five minutes of this, the contact gave up and started to walk back to his office. Karen tried to follow him.

Exasperated, the contact turned on her and ordered her out of the building. Did that faze Karen? Of course not. She figured she could outwit this guy, any day. Karen said to him, "This is too much. I can feel the tension getting to me. If you don't spend the time with me that we agreed to, I am going to have a seizure right here." Her objective: embarrass the guy into sitting down and talking to her.

Isn't that a wonderful way to build up a professional relationship?

It got even worse. The contact said, "I won't do it. Get out of here." Karen then actually fell down on the floor

THE 25 MOST COMMON SALES MISTAKES

and faked a seizure. Two gentlemen from building security had to come and escort her out of the building. Would it surprise you to learn that she didn't get the order?

Perhaps you're laughing at that story. But ask yourself: how many times have you approached it the same way? Do you ever curse under your breath in the middle of a tough cold call? Do you ever persist in calling people who obviously have no use for your product or service? Do you ever walk into a sales appointment fantasizing about how you're going to "nail" a prospect? If you can overcome these habits—and it may take work—you'll distinguish yourself from a lot of bitter, nasty salespeople out there who can't understand why people don't want to talk to them.

We once ordered some copiers for our office. We'd had two bids; the sales rep who lost called and asked why we bought the other machine. I explained in detail why I had made the decision I did; the salesperson didn't agree with my decision, though, and began to yell at me. Didn't I know that the machine had a ninety-day warrantee, free this and free that, half-off such-and-such, and advanced thingamajigs at no extra charge? How on earth could I make a mistake? What was wrong with me?

Needless to say, that exchange didn't change anything. Well, I take that back. It did change something. It made me absolutely secure in my original decision. Obviously, this was not a customer-oriented organization I was dealing with. And I made a mental note never to have anything to do with the Confrontational Copier Company the next time I needed to expand my office copier pool.

Your goal as a salesperson is to create mutual trust; you simply can't do that in an adversarial environment. Be patient. Make repeat visits when necessary. Always listen to what the other person has to say, and accept your prospect's goals as your own. Most important, don't fixate on closing the sale so much that you lose sight of your prospect's dignity.

MISTAKE #5

Getting Distracted

By giving the prospect all your attention, you will, in turn, win the prospect's undivided attention.

Recently, a young salesperson came to my office on an appointment. He went through a rather lengthy discourse about his product; I sat in silence. He came to a point where he had apparently been instructed to ask his prospect a few questions. He asked them dutifully, but somewhat stiffly, as though he were reciting a speech. Time after time, as I began to answer him, I noticed that the salesperson was staring off into space, paying no attention whatsoever to what I was saying. He might as well have been on a coffee break. Perhaps he wished he were.

Many salespeople are so busy running down their checklist of things to do that they forget they're dealing with another human being, and start focusing on things that have nothing to do with the sale.

Part of the reason for that has to do with the stress associated with selling for a living. Often, when confronted with a stressful situation, we'll seal ourselves into a comfortable little world of our own—a world that we can usually control, but that carries with it the very real risk of missing something important.

It's estimated that the average salesperson actually sells for less than five and a half hours a week. In other words, if you're like most salespeople, you're not selling every single hour of every single day. You're doing other things: getting ready to get to see prospects, making your prospecting calls, writing up proposals, attending meetings, filling out paperwork, and so on. That's why it's so vitally important to make every minute you actually spend with a prospect count. Accordingly, you *must* concentrate on what's being said; don't daydream or get sidetracked.

When you get distracted during a sales call, you distract your prospect. You begin to fidget; you wonder what's for lunch; you think about the movie you're going to tonight; you let your mind wander when it shouldn't be wandering. This throws off the whole meeting, because your prospect will sense what's happening, and will wonder what's wrong. The atmosphere of trust won't materialize—and that's bad news. You need that trust.

If you need an incentive, remind yourself that, directly or indirectly, the prospect is telling you the single most important thing you will hear all day: whether or not he or she will buy your product, and why.

Take notes to help you concentrate; make sure your briefcase is well organized, with everything you need at your fingertips. The tools you bring with you to the meeting should help you, not stand in your way. If you find yourself spending five minutes fishing a brochure out of your valise, something's wrong.

The same idea applies to the common problem of attaching too much importance to a confusing or negative remark from the prospect. If the prospect tells you left is right and right is left, don't get befuddled, don't demand an explanation, and by all means don't challenge the person. What will you gain? Ask politely for a clarification if one seems in order, then settle back and pick up from where you left off.

Try to get a bead on the prospect's interests and personality. Ask your basic questions. Then repeat the prospect's ideas. ("So what I'm hearing is that your chief concerns are . . .")

Where appropriate, let the prospect take the lead, and pay attention to what happens next. By isolating factors unique to this particular prospect, you'll remind yourself that you're dealing with another person—one who's important enough to pay close attention to.

MISTAKE #6

Not Taking Notes

As I mentioned briefly earlier, taking proper notes will help you keep the prospect's needs in mind and improve your presentation.

All sales can be broken down into four stages: prospecting, interviewing, presenting, and closing. Perhaps the most crucial stage of the sale is the second one: interviewing. This is where you learn what exactly the prospect's needs and wants are, and whether or not your product or service can help solve a pressing problem. Note-taking is an essential part of this process, and it is an enduring mystery to me why so many people fail to use this basic sales tool.

Assume that I've already worked through the prospecting stage by reaching you through a cold call. Let's say I'm coming to your office now on a sales appointment. You and I meet. We shake hands. You tell me to sit down. I do. You look at me; I look at you. We exchange a little small talk, find out a little bit about one another, and establish some commonality. As the meeting progresses in this way, there will come a moment when you look at me and say, in one form or another, those words that so many sales-people have come to dread.

"Well—what can I do for you?"

That's the point where the real work begins. How I handle that first transition can make or break my sales call. Fortunately, I have a note pad and a pen. And those tools are going to help me establish a solid, professional relationship with you.

In response, I say to you, "Well, Ms. Jones, I work for ABC Widgets. We happen to be the largest manufacturer of widgets on the east coast, and we've worked with about fifteen companies in your industry, including JJ Resources. And the reason I wanted to talk to you today was to find out if there was anything we could do to work together to increase your production. Actually, I had a couple of questions I wanted to ask you about that. Is that all right?"

And I take out my pad and pen. Automatically, I've made a statement. Just by doing that much, I've shown you that I'm professional; I'm organized; I'm in control; and, most important, I'm concerned about your interests (increasing production).

You say, "Sure; go ahead."

And I proceed to ask you about the past, the present, and the future, with regard to your use of widgets.

Note that I don't respond to your "what-can-I-do-for-you" line by talking about how wonderful my Model X Widget is. I can't do that yet. I don't know enough about you. I'm still in the interview stage. So I have to learn more about what it is you need—and get you to talk about yourself and your company—by asking questions and taking notes.

Now here's the interesting part. Anyone who uses this technique for any amount of time will find that prospects talk more when you have a pen and pad out than they will if you just ask them the question point-blank and skip taking notes. Your note-taking reinforces the prospect's desire to speak, and this, of course, gives you more to write. It's a self-perpetuating cycle.

Try it. You'll find it works like nothing else on earth. Why? The fact that I'm taking notes dramatizes my role as an information-gatherer. It makes my job crystal clear to you, the prospect: I am here to learn about your needs.

That's a little bit flattering, isn't it? That shows that I care about what you say and how you look at things, doesn't it? And as long as I'm taking the trouble to write all this down, you'll want to make sure I have the right information about your company and its problems with widgets, won't you?

Because I treat the issue as an important one, you'll agree that it's important for me to know about your widget needs. And you know what? You'll be right. It is important. Getting that information is the only way I can help you solve your problem.

Get the prospect involved; take notes. Use the right tools: a stiff-backed legal pad and a snazzy gold ballpoint pen can make quite an impression. (Fountain pens, though dramatic, can leak and cause your writing to smear.) Stay away from the backs of envelopes or unwieldy pad/portfolio sets; these will detract from the professional image you're trying to present.

Make your prospect feel as important as a movie star giving an interview, or a political candidate holding a press conference. Then use the information you gather to target your approach as you advance to the later stages of the sale.

Failing to Follow Up

When was the last time you wrote a thank-you letter after your first meeting with a prospect?

Many salespeople ignore this crucial step. By taking the time to write a simple, personalized note on company stationery, you help the prospect to remember you—and you put your future sales efforts on a stronger footing.

A friend of mine is a bass fisherman; he told me about a little trick he uses that seems to me to be applicable to sales work. It's pretty simple. When fishing for bass, you must keep the line taut once you get a nibble—otherwise the fish will lose contact with your line and swim away.

A neat, courteous, and professional follow-up letter keeps your line taut—even if it's inappropriate to start reeling in your "fish" right away. Your brief typed note serves as a tactful, professional reminder of your visit, and can reinforce the positive points of your visit.

It can be as simple as, "Dear Jill: Just wanted you to know what a pleasure it was to get to see your plant first-hand. I'll be dropping by with that proposal we discussed on Wednesday as scheduled. I'm quite certain we can work together to increase your widget production. Sincerely, Peter Salesperson."

Why bother? Well, after your initial meeting—even if it went well—you have to ask yourself an important question: what do you think happens in the prospect's mind when you walk out the door?

Do you really imagine that the prospect continues to think about your product, and about how sharp your presentation was, day in and day out? Do you suppose the prospect comes in to work the morning after your visit and thinks, "Gee—how long do I have to wait until I can meet up again with that salesperson I saw yesterday?"

Many salespeople seem to act on this assumption—though what's really likely to happen, even after a spectacular visit with a request for another appointment, is that the prospect will stop a couple of days after your meeting for about three tenths of a second and think, "Now, what's scheduled Wednesday? Oh, yeah—the widget guy. Gotta keep that open."

And that's if you're lucky.

You must keep your line taut—keep your contact fresh—by making the minimal investment of time and care necessary to assemble a short thank-you letter. And, once we accept that, it's simple logic to send follow-up letters at later crucial points of the sale, as well: after a major proposal, for instance—and, of course, after the decision to do business with your company.

At the later stages of the sale, you may move on to handwritten notes, perhaps including interesting clippings from relevant industry publications. Early on, however, you may run the risk of appearing overfamiliar or pretentious by using these techniques. If in doubt, stick with a good typewritten brief letter printed out on sharp company stationery. (Note that it is unnecessary and often excessive to shower a prospect with "little somethings"—a dozen golf balls, say, if you learn the person likes golf.)

Of course, it doesn't hurt to drop your current customers a line now and again, either. I don't know why so many salespeople assume that once a prospect decides to do business with you, no further encouragement is necessary to make that prospect a lifelong customer. Don't make that mistake. Invest five minutes, an envelope, and a stamp, and make a lasting positive impression.

Treating current and prospective customers like professionals worthy of respect is always good business—and follow-up letters are just the tools you need to do that.

Not Keeping in Contact with Past Clients

This ties in neatly with Mistake #7, of course, where we talked about keeping in touch with prospects and current customers. The operative idea here is that someone who decides to use your product or service, and then falls out of your current customer base, is probably still a highly qualified lead.

Help clients keep you in mind. Especially if a significant amount of time has passed (and that may be anywhere from a few months to several years), past clients will often come to a point where they need your product or service again, but don't remember how to get back in touch with you!

When a salesperson calls you for the first time and passes on his or her contact information, do you instantly enter that information in your address book? Probably not. It is usually incumbent upon salespeople to remind potential customers—tactfully and professionally—that the salesperson's company is still out there delivering excellent results. Don't pester people to death, but do give past clients all the facts they need to work with you again.

It's been estimated that you have a one-in-two chance to get business from an existing account, and a one-in-four chance to get business from an old account. When you're prospecting for new customers, the odds drop to one in twenty. Without diminishing for a minute the importance of getting new customers, you can see that keeping in contact with your old clients really does represent significant revenue for you. Keep an organized file of inactive accounts; call or write key people at these companies on a periodic basis. Don't do this in an intrusive or unprofessional way—just keep in touch, as one professional to another.

This approach needn't be an intrusive "hard sell," nor must it proceed at the rapid tempo many salespeople bring to their prospecting work. After all, you already have a relationship with the person. Stay calm, stay friendly, and stay professional. Don't rush things. If the person isn't in a position to buy right now, check back in a month or two.

You may want to set up a simple database system to keep track of your contacts. (By the way, that last sentence originally started "If you have access to and proficiency on a personal computer. . . ." I may have to update these books more often.) Just be sure you're not getting carried away with the process—when you spend more time in front of a computer screen than in front of your prospects, something's wrong. Start small and work your way up.

Don't fall in love with a computer or BlackBerry just because it's a computer or BlackBerry. Make it work for you. Remember that high technology that doesn't help you achieve your goals in a time-sensitive manner isn't really high technology at all—it's probably the wrong technology.

Not Planning the Day Efficiently

Think for a moment about Mistake #1; it has relevance here. You must be absolutely dedicated to getting the very most out of your day, and planning ahead on a daily basis is part of that. Let's face it. Committing to a daily schedule is of paramount importance; your success or failure in this area will have a major impact on your overall performance as a salesperson.

Now, there are a lot of time management books out there. Unfortunately, most of them are so complicated, and take so long to read (let alone implement) that they're virtually worthless for most of today's salespeople. In this section, we'll examine a few brief ideas you can incorporate into your daily routine instantly—so you can start seeing results with the beginning of business tomorrow.

Don't waste hours you could be speaking with clients. Plan your day the evening before.

Prioritize your goals. Don't just start filling out a schedule willy-nilly one evening; make a list of all the things you want to accomplish, then rank them in the order of their importance before you include them on your schedule.

Leave time for crises. Scheduling every day to the brim will cause you to slip from your plan. We all know that strange, unpredictable problems have a way of cropping up from time to time. Leave an hour or so open at the end of the day to manage sudden difficulties. If no crisis arises, you can always move on to your next priority item.

Get up fifteen minutes earlier than you do now—and give yourself a positive charge of energy in the extra time. Starting the day in a rush gets things off to a bad start. Begin the day with a positive affirmation: "This is going to be a great day." Eat a good breakfast. Listen to pleasant music. Stay away from reading or listening to the news first thing in the morning; it's too depressing. Be nice to yourself. (Don't worry, it won't last long.)

Buy and use a doctor's appointment book—the kind with the whole day marked off in fifteen-minute increments. Then keep close watch on the time you spend on any given item. This approach will help you avoid the temptation to allocate vast chunks of your day to vaguely defined goals when you assemble your to-do list.

Also buy a second, smaller book—one that can fit in your pocket or purse. Here you will record what you actually do during the day. Nothing extravagant; just a quick jot-down of the time for each project you undertake as you work through the day. The beauty of this is that you end up with a written record of events, not just your plans, and you can compare the two at day's end. If there's a huge discrepancy between what you plan at 6 p.m. on Tuesday and what you've actually done by 6 p.m.

on Wednesday, you'll know about it and be able to work on it. If you're like most salespeople, you'll probably realize, in doing this, just how much time you spend on the road. Chances are that you'll acquire a new enthusiasm for scheduling quality appointments. You'll also have hard evidence of your own habits—lunch at a certain time, so many calls in the morning, so much down time between meetings, etc. By knowing these "givens," your daily planning will become much more effective.

On Friday evening, prepare not only your Monday morning schedule, but also your thumbnail sketch of the week to come. Odds are that this will take the form primarily of meetings and other commitments; don't feel you have to account for every minute of every one of the next five days. Just block out your scheduled appointments and meetings so you have a good solid overview of what's on the horizon. Where appropriate, leave yourself "into-and-out-of" time. After all, you know that you won't simply materialize out of thin air at your three o'clock appointment across town, but will have to drive there, leaving early enough to assure arrival ten minutes or so before three.

By attending to daily scheduling matters conscientiously, and comparing your actual results with your plan, you'll increase your time-effectiveness and lay solid foundations for your sales success.

Not Looking Your Best

Some years back, I worked for a successful Broadway publicist and promoter who had an interesting habit.

Every day, after lunch with a client, he would come back to the office and, before going into his next appointment, he'd step into the restroom, spruce himself up, and change his shirt. He'd tackle the second half of the day looking just as polished and confident as he had at eight-fifteen that morning.

Now, I'm not suggesting you go out and expand your work wardrobe by a factor of two. It's the mindset I want you to look at. After all, if you're like me, you've probably seen plenty of salespeople wander through an afternoon with crooked ties, mussed-up hair, and the spaghetti sauce from lunch emblazoned on their chests.

If you're a prospect, you remember someone who walks in the door looking sharp. Such a salesperson makes an instant positive impression, and has already done a lot to win respect and trust in those crucial first seconds. So check yourself out in the restroom before each and every sales appointment; you might even carry a compact mirror with you for those times you can't reach the facilities. Look sharp.

A salesperson I know started out at his new job looking just that way—sharp. But as the months went by, and as he became a little more familiar with the routine, he started coming in wearing his "B" shirts now and then. You know what a "B" shirt (or blouse or skirt) is: a little frayed, a little worn, a bit threadbare at the edges, but good enough to get by with if people don't look too close.

Your prospect will be looking close.

Don't let the fact that you do what you do every day fool you into thinking that your prospect deals with the same repetition. Each prospect you encounter is an exciting new opportunity, and should be treated as such. You wouldn't walk into a job interview wearing a "B" shirt; don't walk into a sales call showing anything less than your best.

When it comes to work, stay away from any piece of clothing that doesn't instantly communicate your status as an intelligent, organized professional. Save the casual wear for off-hours. Keep in mind that, for a salesperson who meets people regularly, who lives or dies by first impressions, there are certain things that simply have to look impeccable: fingernails, hair, shoes, clothing.

Failing to look sharp just leaves an opening for the next salesperson who does. Don't give up that competitive edge. Show the world your best side, every day.

Not Keeping Sales Tools Organized

Your professional image, as we've seen, depends to a large degree on your personal appearance. However, you should also keep in mind that it depends on your tools as well.

What do you suppose goes through the mind of a prospect who, upon meeting a salesperson, sees all sorts of objects tumble randomly from his or her opened briefcase?

Your briefcase should give the impression of order and precision when opened. It should not be overflowing with laundry lists, last week's newspapers, dirty ties, bills, or food.

It should contain: your legal pad; your business cards; your pens; appropriate product materials and/or samples; a handheld calculator; and perhaps your pocket-sized datebook. That's it.

Often, salespeople will bring too much to an appointment. You don't need everything in the building to talk to a single prospect, and even though carting along reams of samples and brochures may make you feel more secure on the way to the appointment, you're likely to look confused and befuddled as you paw through it all trying to find the material you want.

Obviously, if your type of selling demands a display of a tangible product, you'll need to incorporate that element, perhaps with a smart-looking sample case. But stay away from the fancy flipcharts and display boxes and framed testimonials. They're virtually always more trouble than they're worth. Usually, the only thing you can count on from all this extraneous material is a less confident, poised presentation.

If you find that you're going to your appointments so weighed down with samples and display cases that you're exhausted from the minute you walk in the door, you will eventually have to make a change somewhere. If it's agony for you to carry all that, it will be agony for the prospect to look at you. Try to pinpoint the prospect's areas of concern; you can always bring requested material on your second visit.

As we will learn a little later in this book, business can be compared, in many respects, to war. Both require strategy, planning, competition, intelligence, and so forth. If you think of your sales work in that way, you'll see that your sales tools are really part of your ammunition. As such, they should be maintained with care and respect.

Not Taking the Prospect's Point of View

Get to know your product or service thoroughly, isolating how it helps people; only in this way can you apply your knowledge to the prospect's needs.

Salespeople usually know that they should outline product features: those constant, intrinsic elements the item presents. Someone selling a tin can might call attention to the fact that it's curved along the edges, and that it holds a certain amount of material. A fountain pen, in the same manner, can be said to have a point, or to write with ink. This book might be highlighted by pointing out that it's a certain number of pages long, or that it's rectangular.

All true. And all very boring.

Features are essential—no one wants to buy a fountain pen that does not have a point—but features are not usually the first thing on the prospect's mind. Typically, the prospect will be concerned with a different idea entirely: benefit. And this, too, must be emphasized by the salesperson.

Benefits are what the user will get out of an item. A tin can, when considered by a food processing firm, might be said to have a benefit if its design allows more cans of soup to be produced in a given day than the design of a competing can. Someone considering buying a fountain pen might isolate a benefit by noticing that one brand's ink cartridges are easier to load than another brand's. And someone comparing this book to another book on sales might notice that it's broken into brief, easy-to-read chapters—an important factor for a salesperson who's pressed for time.

What about your product or service? What benefits can you isolate? What tangible advantages do your customers have over the customers of the competition?

Once you begin to see things from this perspective— the potential customer's perspective—you'll be able to start assembling the key selling points of your product or service. It is a common mistake to concentrate instead on features, and subject the prospect to a barrage of confusing technical information of limited interest.

Think about how you approach buying something. Your main concern is not how the lawnmower, refrigerator, or automobile was assembled in the first place, but rather how the whole conglomerate will help you mow your lawn, get ice when you need it, or achieve good gas mileage.

If the salesperson focuses on those goals of yours, he or she will be speaking your language—and will be able to communicate essential facts about the product.

If, on the other hand, the salesperson starts talking about rigid-comb titanium construction with DL-X latex bearing modules, you're going to smile, nod politely, and pretend you understand what's being said. Unfortunately, though, you won't be any closer to knowing what you want to know about the product.

You should, if at all possible, actually use the product or service as a customer would. Research your product or service thoroughly from the prospect's point of view; isolate benefits. Then you'll be able to make crystal clear the advantages your prospect will have by choosing you.

Not Taking Pride in Your Work

Some years back, I went to do a program at a major consumer products company. During a question-and-answer period, I asked the participants to call out the reasons their company should be considered number one in its field.

I stood there in front of the flip chart, marker in hand, waiting. No response. After a little while, a hand went up. "Yes?" I asked. "You know, Steve," the man said (and I'm paraphrasing him here), "we may be number one on raxilated widgets, but when it comes to looking at world mid-sized widget production, I think we actually rank around number four."

"No," a woman called out from the back of the room. "No, six. Mid-sized widgets, we just got the new rankings, we're sixth."

"Sixth," said the man.

Another pause.

"Okay, well that's interesting to know," I said. "Anything else? What is there that really makes this company great? Anyone?"

A man in the front row cleared his throat.

"Yes?"

"The new cafeteria," he said slowly, "is certainly nice."

Just then, a younger fellow asked to be recognized.

"Yes? What is it about this company that really gets you going?"

He looked surprised. "What?" he asked. "Oh, no, I just wanted to say something. Mort mentioned the cafeteria. They've had some plumbing problems, I just thought I'd let everyone know it's out of commission this week."

"Then I take back," said Mort, "what I said about the cafeteria."

"You know what bugs me," said a young lady on my right, "is the way they changed the pay schedules around. We used to get reviews annually, on January first. Now they're doing it by your anniversary date with the company, which means I'll get a raise six weeks later this year."

You see my point. The group I was addressing had not taken it as an article of faith that one should take pride in one's organization. Instead, when asked to list positive aspects of their work environment, they either put forward petty complaints or said nothing at all.

That's not the way to make your company number one, and that's not the way to make yourself number one, either.

If you can't stand behind what you do and where you do it with every fiber of your being, why bother? Why punch a clock? Why show up in the morning? Why do something that, clearly, you do not enjoy doing? Why ask people to buy your product or service if you don't believe in it?

If you don't take pride in your product or service, and in the organization that stands behind it, you will not be successful. If you focus only on the negatives, the obstacles, the reasons you can't sell the way you should—guess what? You won't sell the way you should.

Pinpoint factors that mark you as superior to your competition. Become comfortable discussing those factors in an optimistic way. In short, talk your organization up. Don't just do this at work, though it's certainly essential there, but mention where you work and why it's great at parties, social gatherings, conventions—everywhere. (By the way, this will not only build your optimism about the business, but also expose you to a whole new universe of potential customers.)

Now then. Suppose you have a real problem with your company. Suppose the reason you don't feel great about where you work goes beyond normal sales cycles or standard management headaches, and is instead rooted in some legitimate, deep-seated objection. Like you have a moral problem selling what you sell. Or a supervisor engages in persistent, subtle (or maybe not-so-subtle) sexual harassment. Or the quotas you must meet are so high that the whole staff burns out on a regular basis, and turnover is always high.

Does any of that mean you shouldn't be enthusiastic about where you work?

No. It means you *should* be enthusiastic about where you work, but you should work somewhere else.

If you can't get behind the program 100 percent, find somewhere you can—then give it everything you've got. Be proud of where you work, and what you do for a living. You'll see that results will soon follow.

Trying to Convince, Rather Than Convey

When you really want to make a sale—I mean, desperately want to make a sale—it's easy to slip into a "convincing" mode. You'll corner the prospect, you'll review why your product or service is great, you'll get past all the troublesome objections, and finally, the prospect will see the light of day and buy from you.

The only problem is, it's exactly the opposite of what you have to do. You have to commit to understanding the problems and concerns of the prospect, not steamrolling over them. And you have to work from there to show—to demonstrate in a compelling way—how your product or service can address the relevant concerns.

In short, you have to convey value and benefit, rather than convince the prospect that his or her concerns are unfounded. Remember: it's always better to let the prospect do the talking, and act on the concerns he or she expresses, than to do all the talking yourself and expect a yes answer.

I know it's important for you to make sales. That's the whole idea behind the work I do, and behind every word of this book. But most successful salespeople come to realize that being anxious to close a sale, and working like crazy to get the prospect to see your point of view, are only going to decrease your odds of closing.

Sales is not about getting other people to see your point of view. It's about getting you to see things from other people's points of view. If you are committed to helping your prospect solve a problem, "convincing" is irrelevant. The issue is not changing someone's mind, but conveying to the person exactly why and how you can help solve a pressing problem. And you have to see and understand that problem before you can hope to solve it.

That is not to say that high-pressure, manipulative selling does not exist. It does. But think of how you felt the last time you had something "rammed down your throat" by a high-pressure salesperson. Did it make you feel better about the company the salesperson worked for? Did it make you want to go back again for another purchase? Did it make you want to recommend the company to others?

The important question for you to ask yourself is this: are you interested in developing a sales career, or are you interested in developing one sale?

When people have been overwhelmed by a salesperson, when they feel doubts about the wisdom of a purchase decision, when they're afraid they may have been cheated, they say, "Some salesperson sold me this." When people really feel good about a product, they say, "I bought this." That's the difference between a one-time sale and a good solid customer. Which would you rather have?

Build trust. Emphasize past successes. Highlight solutions to problems. By doing this you'll convey the points necessary to get the prospect to make the right decisions.

Underestimating the Prospect's Intelligence

It's not uncommon to hear a salesperson say something like, "You know, the prospect I met with today was so dumb—he had no idea what I was talking about." Maybe you've even heard yourself making remarks like that. My question to you is, what does that say about you as a salesperson? You are a conveyor of information. You are a conduit. You are the connecting unit between your business and the end user.

How can a prospect know the ins and outs of your business before you explain anything? And why, for that matter, should that prospect need to know more about your business than your phone number, anyway?

There is one area, though, that the prospect has a great deal of knowledge about—knowledge you need. And that area is his or her problems. Remember, solving customer problems is what sales is all about, and you will—or should—spend a great deal of time trying to ferret out information from your prospects. Considering all that effort, it doesn't really make sense to proceed on the assumption that the prospect doesn't know anything. Clearly the prospect does know something important, otherwise you wouldn't set up meetings to try to learn that something.

Your job is to learn the problems the prospect is having, then show how your product or service can be used to competitive advantage in solving those problems. You must approach this task as the prospect's partner and as an equal. If you bring arrogance or a superior attitude to the appointment, that will show through, and your sales will suffer.

The prospect doesn't know your product or service as well as you do because he or she doesn't sell it for a living. You do, and you should be able to provide essential information immediately, not shake your head in disappointment that the prospect isn't catching on as quickly as you'd like.

You can encourage the efficient flow of information between yourself and your prospect by being scrupulously honest with the prospect about your company and what it has to offer. Acting otherwise can cause big problems. I was working with a company that produces industrial machinery recently; one of their sales reps was indignant that her prospects had "lied" to her about the status of forthcoming orders. As it happened, this rep's whole approach to customers was flip, glib, and, on the whole, disrespectful. My guess is that she herself was not completely honest in dealing with her prospects. Is it any wonder she got bad information back from them?

As long as you and your prospect, working together, can define the problem to a degree sufficient for you to be of help, the prospect is quite intelligent enough. Your goal is not to dwell on what you consider to be the prospect's shortcomings, but rather to encourage an extremely intelligent decision: that of doing business with your firm.

MISTAKE #16

Not Keeping Up to Date

Knowledge is power.

Suppose you walked in to see a current customer for an appointment, and your contact had lost an arm since you'd last seen him. Would you notice?

Granted, something that obvious probably wouldn't get past you. However, there are clues and tipoffs that are, from the point of view of the prospect's business, just as blunt—clues that are visible from the moment you walk in the door, but that many salespeople miss.

What is going on in the businesses of your clients? Do you know? If there were a major layoff in the offing, would you hear about it? Is the business doing well? Is a merger in the works? Are key people happy with your product or service, or is it something a budget-cutter might consider expendable?

Too many salespeople tend to think of "closed sales" as static things, and very little in business is static. The sad truth is, no business exists for the sole purpose of purchasing your product or service. If your customers do well, you will do well—and, conversely, if they do poorly, you will do poorly. Whatever the case, it is to your advantage to have accurate information ahead of time.

Observing the prospect closely, making an effort to understand exactly what's happening at his or her business (and why), will help you gain a broader outlook on the whole environment in which your company operates.

Of course, watching your prospects firsthand isn't the only weapon at your disposal. There are innumerable reports, journals, and newsletters available to you—and if you have many clients in a given industry, it's a good idea to keep up with that industry's trade news.

A salesperson I know named Marcia had been trying to get in touch with someone at a large company with regard to her company's courier service. She was getting nowhere, and when her contact asked her to "send along some information," she was convinced that she'd reached a dead end. Still, she dutifully mailed the information, but nothing happened for weeks on end. She wrote the account off.

Six months later, she received a call from her contact at the firm. Could she come in for an appointment right away? She could; and did; and made a big sale. Curiosity got the better of her, though, and at the end of the meeting she came right out and asked: why had they waited so long to respond? The answer: the company's main competitor had begun a new program earlier that year that required courier service. They were getting in on it now, and wished they had known about what their rivals were up to earlier.

The moral, of course, is that had Marcia been able to keep up with industry publications and/or gossip, she might well have been able to tell her contact how a courier service was working out for others in the industry—and closed the account months earlier.

Who does your prospect sell to? Who are your prospect's competitors? How do these competitors sell? What are the main differences between the products and prices of your prospect's firm and its competitors? What is the prospect's market share? What is the prospect's perceived market share? How does your prospect plan to deal with new obstacles? New opportunities? Are any new technological breakthroughs on the horizon? How do all these factors affect decisions about whether or not to buy from you?

Avoid needlessly complex and drawn-out research, but keep your eyes and ears open, and read essential publications. The more you know, the better off you'll be.

Rushing the Sale

I mentioned a little earlier that there are four steps to every sale. We'll look more closely at those four steps here. No matter what you sell or where you sell it, your sale can typically be broken down into the following stages: qualifying, interviewing, presentation, and closing. Let's examine each stage individually.

Qualifying. Also called prospecting or cold calling, this is where you contact someone you've never spoken to before (often by calling them on the phone) and determining that there is a possible use for your product or service. You may set up an appointment or future call date at this stage.

Interviewing. You learn the past, present, and future with regard to the prospect's use of your product or service. You find out what special problems have presented themselves recently. You learn other pertinent facts about the prospect.

Presentation. You show exactly how your product or service can help solve the problems identified during the interview stage. You appeal to past successes with other customers.

Closing. You ask for the sale.

It's possible that you can proceed through all four stages in a single telephone call. It's also possible that it will take you months or even years of appointments and follow-up appointments to go from making your cold call to reaching and completing the final stage. All that depends on the product or service you offer, your industry, its customers, the prevailing economic conditions—a number of different factors.

At any given point in the cycle, your objective is to move from where you are to the next stage. In other words, if you are qualifying, your goal is to move on to interviewing; if you are interviewing, you want to get to a point where the prospect is comfortable with a presentation, and so on. There is one rule, though, that you must bear in mind in considering the cycles I've outlined above. The rule is a simple one: the simplest and most reliable way to lose a sale is to move from one stage to the next before the prospect is ready to do so.

Many salespeople view their work as one gigantic closing stage. By failing to understand the cyclical nature of their work with a prospect, they rush things, and, accordingly, lose sales.

Let's say you have a garden. One morning you walk out into your garden and sow seeds for a tomato plant.

If you're a smart gardener, you'll realize that it's going to take most of the summer for the tomato to make it from the seed stage into your salad bowl. If you wait a couple of weeks, see something vaguely tomato-like emerge from the ground, rip it up, and smother it with vinaigrette dressing, it's not going to make for a very good (or even edible) salad.

If, however, you give it time, and let it mature, it will blossom into a juicy, ripe tomato. Then you can brag about it. But if you rush the process, you're not going to get anything for your efforts.

Selling is just the same. There are certain things for which you simply must wait; otherwise you're not in the sales business, you're in the rejection business. You're a professional collector of rejections.

You should not attempt to walk into an office for the first time, shake hands with a prospect, and ask when the operations department would like to receive the first order. In this instance, you are attempting to rush from the interview stage into the closing stage, and your results will be disastrous. Most problems of rushing, however, are not that obvious. Perhaps you've talked a little bit about yourself, mentioned your product, admired the view, gotten a little past history, and received an assurance that what you're talking about "sounds interesting."

Are you ready to move on to the presentation stage? Maybe—and maybe not. The best option is usually to ask the prospect straight out: "Well, is there anything else you think I should know about your company, Mr. Smith?"

Depending on the answer you get, you'll be able to gauge the prospect's enthusiasm for moving on to the next stage. When in doubt, err on the side of patience. There's no crime in saying, "Well, I've learned a lot about your company today; what I'd like to do now is set up an appointment for next week so I can go over a completed proposal with you."

(*Note:* The complex issue of managing your sales cycle is covered in detail in my book *Sales Presentation Techniques.*)

Not Using People Proof

What is people proof?

"Mr. Jones, I know this program will work for you, and I'll tell you why. We had a company in your industry, ABC Tires, that was very skeptical about what we said we could do for them. But they did try the program, and we did in fact deliver the results. And I know that the same thing can happen here with your firm."

That's people proof, and it's some of the most powerful ammunition at your disposal. People proof reinforces positive inclinations toward your company, and gives people a logical reason to confirm the emotional decision to do business with you. If you can cite another business (or, better still, another business in the same industry) that's had success with the product or service you're offering now, you're well on the way toward building the trust and confidence necessary to close the sale.

Many salespeople react badly when I make this suggestion. They say, "Steve, it won't work for me; I work in an industry where confidentiality is important."

I've got news for you. Everyone works in an industry where confidentiality is important.

It's a simple enough matter to clear such informal use of client names ahead of time. After all, you're not giving away company secrets—just disclosing the fact that you worked for a certain firm. You do the same thing when you type up a client list.

Just mention to your contact at ABC Tires that you'd like to be able to include his company (and perhaps even his name, if he's agreeable) in your literature and personal presentations. Keep the atmosphere casual and friendly; don't make it appear that your customer is making any kind of commitment to you. You may be surprised at the results. The normal customer reaction is to be flattered, not paranoid.

People proof works wonders. It makes you less of an untested quantity, and more of a proven problem-solver. It builds legitimacy in the eyes of the prospect, and helps you get down to the important business of solving problems through your product or service.

Humbling Yourself

You are a professional. There's no need for you to abase yourself or fawn over a prospect rather than work with the person to solve a problem. Doing so usually has a negative—rather than positive—effect on your sales efforts.

At a program I was conducting a while back, I made a recommendation to a salesperson named Myra that she not only try to meet with her contact at a certain company, but also attempt to set up a meeting with the head of the firm. She was shocked at this suggestion.

"Oh, Steve," she said. "I can't do that."

"Why not?" I asked.

"Well," she explained, "if I ask my contact to put me in touch with the president, the answer might be no. Then where would I be with my contact?"

There's a new idea, don't you think? A salesperson being confronted with the word "no"—certainly a unique event in the daily life of a salesperson, and certainly an excellent reason not to try something in the first place.

Myra, I learned, was not with the company three months later. Why not? Well, think about it. That exchange she and I had said a lot about the way she looked at her contact—and at sales as a profession. She was petrified at the idea of offending her contact, and my guess is that it was because she believed, deep down, that the contact was doing her a favor by giving her business.

In short, she relinquished control of her sales environment, and humbled herself to contacts. Her thinking probably ran something like this: if I'm nice enough to Mrs. Jones, if I take her out to lunch every week, if I remember her kids' names and birthdates, if I never give her a reason to have a free, open, give-and-take discussion with me—if I can do all that, maybe, just maybe, I'll get on her good side enough for her to buy a widget from me.

Something's missing there, don't you think?

Where does Mrs. Jones's company's need for widgets come in? And where does Myra's role as conduit and facilitator come in?

My guess is that Myra could not see herself as a professional—as a partner. Instead, the Myras of this world tend to see themselves as supplicants.

Are you a professional? Or are you still in the process of trying to gain professional respect from your prospects? The paradox is that the very act of trying too hard to gain that respect will turn people off to what you have to say.

How you look at yourself, of course, has a great deal to do with how others look at you. This is why a commitment to ongoing motivational work is so terribly important.

No one's saying sales is easy. No one's saying you'll never get rejected. And no one's saying there won't be days where, despite all your best efforts, you feel like you're simply not getting anything accomplished.

Nevertheless, you must find an internal reservoir of strength, confidence, and security in your identity as a professional, and you must convey all that to your prospect—as an equal. Because that's what you are.

You must operate from the assumption that you bring to the table a specific set of skills and a level of product knowledge that the other person can benefit from. If you operate on the opposite assumption, that the person across the table from you has a prize that you can win if only you can prove yourself worthy to him or her, you're in trouble. The only people you're going to win over (if you're lucky) are extremely insecure prospects—and those people are not the ones who tend to achieve the highest levels of success in business.

When you stop to think about it, my bet is that you'll see that the people you'll most want to work with (and emulate) have a strong sense of self, of confidence, and of professionalism—and have every expectation of the same from you.

Don't let them down.

Being Fooled by "Sure Things"

There's a saying in baseball about never taking your eye off the ball. The same advice applies to salespeople who get so excited about a big sale they think is all but sewed up that they lose sight of the rest of their prospect base.

There's nothing wrong with a little healthy enthusiasm, but when you spend hours (or days) dreaming about how you're going to spend the money you'll pick up from the Kilgore deal, watch out. Those dreams are costing you money, because they're nibbling away at time you should be spending developing new customers. Those dreams are letting you justify being complacent; and complacency is something a good salesperson can't afford, no matter how good things on the horizon look.

Daydreams on the job are troubling enough, but what's even more disturbing is when salespeople make a big deal out of potential sales that really aren't that promising. We move here beyond simple complacency and into outright self-deception. I'd like to be able to say here that such problems are rare, but unfortunately they're all too common.

And it's not that difficult to see why. Salespeople thrive on hope. When you've been turned down all day long, it's very tempting to treat the first nibble you get as The Big One You've Been Waiting For. However, you can gain some vitally important perspective by thinking a little bit more deeply about your sales cycle.

What I'm about to outline is something that can, for some people, turn an entire sales career around. For others, it will take years of misplaced efforts and untold frustration to realize fully the implications of the seven simple words I'm about to pass along.

You make money when someone says "no."

How is that possible? How on earth can you expect to make money by hearing a prospect tell you he's not interested?

Easy.

Let's say you make twenty contact calls a day. Of the twenty decision-makers you reach, not everyone is going to want to make an appointment with you. You don't walk to your desk, pick up the phone, and expect twenty appointments from twenty calls out of yourself. You're smarter than that.

You expect, say, five appointments. Of those five appointments, you can expect to close perhaps one sale. (These ratios can vary from industry to industry and from salesperson to salesperson, but you get the idea.)

Let's say that you get a $200 commission on that sale. Now, most salespeople tend to think of all the work that went into that sale—the calling, the appointments, and so on—as some sort of administrative hassle that it would be nice to be able to avoid. They see the work that precedes the sale as a technicality, and spend all their efforts trying to zoom in on that one big call that simply equals $200.

But that's not really the way it works, is it? In fact, you do have to make those twenty calls in order to have the five appointments that lead you to the sale. And, when you think about it, if you cut those calls in half, and only make ten every day instead of twenty, you'll be cutting your sales in half, won't you?

In short, every call you make, and every appointment you go on, is part of your personal sales cycle—including the rejections!

You could even look at it this way: for every contact call you make, you "earn" $10, even if the contact says, "No thank you, we're already using ABC Widgets because my brother-in-law works there and he gives them to me for free, so please don't ever call again."

Now, with this perspective, you can see that having one big sale, while certainly nice, isn't going to do you much good in terms of your long-term overall cycle—because you're going to want new sales next month, and the month after that. And you can also see that, if the Big One doesn't come through, that's disappointing, but really no problem if you put adequate effort in on both ends of the cycle—the twenty calls and the one close. There will be other Big Ones waiting for you down the line.

Keep your eye on the ball—and don't get fooled by "sure things."

Taking Rejection Personally

Having discussed, in the previous chapter, how you make money when someone says "no," we're in a good position to look more closely at the whole issue of rejection and how salespeople react to it.

For a salesperson, as we've seen, a rejection is not a personal affront, but rather part of the overall cycle inherent in any day's work.

Salespeople simply must learn to look at the issue in this way. After all, there's only one sure-fire way to avoid rejection—though it does work like a charm. That way is never to ask for anything. Don't ask for the appointment; don't ask for the sale; don't try to show your prospect how you can help solve problems. You'll never get rejected. Unfortunately, you'll never make any money, either.

One man I worked with recently, Frank, was trying to make the transition from work as an administrator to a job as a field sales representative. He went into the new position with high hopes. After all, he was a people person. He loved talking about his product. And he knew it inside and out.

However, he was not prepared for the amount of work he had to do to make his efforts worthwhile. He learned in short order that, to get to a realistic number of "yes" answers, he had to be willing to listen to a lot of "no" answers. And that was tough for him.

Frank had worked for fifteen years in a totally different environment. He had grown used to working for weeks on a proposal, having that proposal passed around and returned to him with suggestions, and then putting together another draft—a draft everyone believed in.

Now he was asking himself to move from that slow, consensus-oriented job to a rapid-fire, binary, on-or-off world that profoundly confused him.

He said to me, "Steve, it's not a matter of my not knowing that rejection is part of the cycle. I know how many people I have to see to make money; that's how many people I see. And I'm doing all right. But I'm completely stressed out. I guess it's more a problem of me believing that when people turn down my product, they're really turning me down. And that's hard for me to adjust to at this point. I wish I could change the way I look at things; I know I've tried."

Ultimately, Frank decided that sales wasn't for him; and looking back on it, I'd have to agree with him.

Now, I'm not telling you this story to convince you that if you don't like rejection, you should get out of sales. Nobody likes rejection, and it's natural to feel some disappointment when you hear someone say "no."

But the crucial issue is how you deal with that rejection. If you can teach yourself to accept that the fact that the person says "no" is not a reflection on you, your product, or your company, but merely in the course of things, you can dust yourself off and move on to the next prospect.

But if, over time, it's impossible for you to teach yourself that, then a career in sales is going to be very difficult for you. There's a good chance you'll even start to take out the stress you feel on prospects who have no intention of rejecting you. If that happens with any regularity, there is very little chance for you to succeed.

Unfortunately, not everyone is cut out for a career in sales. Some people, like Frank, simply have so much invested in other work modes that a change really isn't a realistic option. For others, fortunately, it's possible to pick up the resilience and self-assurance necessary to approach the issue of rejection from a detached, professional point of view.

Whether you realize it now or not, the main obstacle in approaching the issue of rejection is not how the prospect thinks of you, but how you think of yourself. Don't be too hard on yourself; accept steady progress happily. If you can eventually make the necessary adjustments, and not take rejection personally, you'll be on your way to sales success.

Not Assuming Responsibility

This chapter may look like a direct contradiction to the last one, but as you'll see, it's not. Assuming personal responsibility is really a proven method for getting your prospect to pass along important information.

A wonderful salesperson I'll call Joe works for a major security guard firm in the Midwest. Joe is seventy-two years old, and has been with this company since 1964. If you ask Joe to talk to you about his firm, he'll tell you with complete sincerity and the utmost pride that he works for the number one security firm in the United States of America, bar none.

When Joe is on a sales visit, and he comes to the closing stage of his meeting, he'll ask his prospect when the best time would be for the security service to start. Two things can happen. The prospect can be receptive, in which case Joe will take down all the relevant information on a form and set up a starting date for the service. And, of course, the prospect can back off and say no. That's when something very interesting happens.

If the prospect says no, Joe is shocked and somewhat taken aback. It's not an act; he believes in his company so completely, and ends up knowing so much about his prospect by the time he suggests a purchase, that he is legitimately concerned if he hears a negative decision.

Here's what Joe says: "Mr. Smith, I don't know what to say. I am so convinced that we have the best service, the best pricing, the best site customization, and the best reputation of any security guard service in the country that I can only think of one reason for you not to sign on with us. And that's that I must have done something terribly wrong just now in giving my presentation to you. I'm going to ask you to help me out, Mr. Smith, and show me where I went off course, because, to tell you the truth, I know this service is right for you, and I would really hate to have fouled things up."

What do you think the prospect says?

It's pretty difficult to come back with your standard "Gee, Joe, it's just not really right for us" response after all that, isn't it? If you're Mr. Smith, you probably respect Joe quite a bit for believing in what he does so strongly, and for putting himself on the line in that way. So you aren't going to mumble something vague and useless to Joe. You're going to give him what he needs—information on where there's a problem.

Typically, what Joe hears at this point is, "No, no, no, it's not you, Joe, it's nothing you did. It's on our end." And the prospect will go into detail about the remaining obstacles. Then Joe has the information he needs to continue working with the prospect.

I suppose I don't have to tell you that Joe is the most successful salesperson in that organization. By putting aside the idea that he must always be perceived as having done the "right" thing, Joe achieves important objectives: he opens up the prospect, illuminates remaining problems, and begins working to solve them.

You can do exactly the same thing.

Underestimating the Importance of Prospecting

As you've probably gathered by this point, I place a tremendous amount of importance on the act of prospecting for new customers. There's a good reason for this. A solid commitment to prospecting is the one habit that, if developed correctly, is most likely to ensure sales success.

You can have problems keeping up with technical advancements. You can stumble occasionally during in-person presentations. You can work in an incredibly competitive industry. But if you prospect effectively, you can compensate for these problems—and be quite successful in spite of them.

Part of the problem is that salespeople tend to look at prospecting in general (and cold calling in particular) as a chore to be avoided. As we've seen, avoiding the prospecting stage is senseless; prospecting is the first, crucial stage in the development of new customers.

"But," you may be saying to yourself, "I don't need new customers. I just closed six accounts. I'm going to get repeat business from them. I'm all set."

Wrong.

You may think you're all set for now (and many sales-people in this situation do think that), but you are not all set for next month, or the month after that, or next year. Even if things do look great right now.

We all know that sales is an up-and-down endeavor. There are good months and bad months. It's the nature of the beast. Far too many of the "downs" salespeople experience, however, are preventable. These slumps often result not from seasonal dips in business or economic decline on a large scale, but from the failure of salespeople to make sure that they have prospects in the pipeline at all times.

A friend of mine who was working for a large insurance company was doing extremely well. One year he took in nearly $200,000 in commissions, and established himself as the star of the staff. One day, though, he called me. His voice was tense, and I could tell something was the matter.

"Steve," he said, "I'm in trouble. I wasn't prospecting."

Star of the staff or no star of the staff, my friend had dug himself into a hole. He'd gotten cocky. He'd made a lot of money, but he'd spent most of it on fancy vacations and expensive toys. He'd neglected his prospect base for the better part of a year, had developed no new clients, and was now watching his income drop precipitously month by month. He was working like crazy just to make up lost ground.

You're never so successful that you can ignore prospecting. You never have a base of clients that's big enough to last forever.

Most salespeople are well advised to make a certain number of cold calls every day, no matter what. I recommend talking to twenty decision-makers. Whatever number you settle on, make prospecting part of your routine; block it off in your schedule.

Keep something in the pipeline all the time; you'll regret it if you don't.

(For more information on prospecting skills, see my book *Cold Calling Techniques That Really Work!*)

MISTAKE #24

Focusing on Negatives

I've worked with many salespeople, and I've come to the conclusion that there are some people who simply spend their whole careers inventing and/or reinforcing obstacles.

Everyone's seen this in action: the water cooler gripe sessions, the behind-the-back gossiping, the snide remarks on off-days. The potential topics are innumerable. Office politics. Perceived defects in the product or service. Impossibly tough competition. Endless personal problems. Unfair commission schedules.

As that noted sales trainer Roseanne Roseannadanna might have put it, it's always something.

Now don't get me wrong. We all have problems, every single day. But some people enter the ring half-beaten, and some enter considering the battle half won. A successful salesperson must fall into the latter category; a persistent negative outlook will not only make it difficult for coworkers and supervisors to work with you—it will make it difficult for prospects to work with you.

It's common for me to hear a salesperson complain, "Steve, you don't understand how much is expected of us here." My feeling is that most of the time, this is nothing more than a martyr act on the part of the salesperson. I've met with hundreds upon hundreds of sales managers, and their goals are usually pretty clear-cut: get good results from the staff. Not necessarily walking-on-water results, but at least keeping-your-head-above-water results. (It's interesting to note that most of the people who complain about how high their quotas are complain only during dry spells; if business is good, the same quota can be considered quite manageable.)

If you're not making sales, complaining about everything in sight is only going to compound your problem. Not only will you be wasting valuable time you could be using to talk to new prospects, but you'll also lose perspective you need to identify and resolve the problems you're having.

Many companies have had the experience of having a salesperson perform poorly in a certain territory, complaining that "the market is saturated" within it. Take that person off the territory, put someone else on it, and—shazam!—sales take off, saturation or no saturation. The difference? Usually, the first salesperson fixates on limitations, while the new rep brings no preconceptions to the work, and sees fresh opportunities as a result.

Selling is difficult work; no one is saying it isn't. But you must be able to isolate problems, deal with them, and then get down to business. Remember, your workplace is where you must *work toward making sales*. Doing anything else—specifically, letting yourself get caught up in negative diversions—is simply giving away your competitive edge.

Stay positive. Stay upbeat. You are your own greatest asset; focusing on negatives keeps you from performing at your peak.

Not Showing Competitive Spirit

In my view, if you are a salesperson, you are a member of an army, and your army is at war. Fortunately, this type of war presents a great advantage over the standard type: nobody dies in it. But that fact doesn't diminish by a single millimeter the importance of a competitively oriented winning spirit; nor does it decrease your need, and your company's need, for sound battlefield strategies and tactics.

Too many salespeople think of themselves as being loners, being on their own. In fact, your company has made an immense investment in you, and will succeed or fail on the battlefield, in large measure, based on your performance and the performance of your coworkers. You share with a number of other people a common goal: success for your firm. To the degree that your company succeeds, you will succeed; to the degree that your company fails, you will fail.

You're not alone. You're on the front lines, fighting for customers, and the fight is a serious one. If you or your company doesn't take it seriously, you'll lose customers to competitors and eventually "die"—i.e., go out of business.

You must be absolutely dedicated to victory in gaining and keeping satisfied customers, because there is almost certainly someone else out there who wants those customers just as badly as you do. That someone will fight for your business, and fight to diminish your success as a salesperson in your company. You must act aggressively to keep this from occurring.

People often accuse me of being overdramatic when I make this point, but whenever they do, I just tell them that if being overdramatic works for the Chinese, it might just help us out as well. For these are the principles by which the Chinese have guided their industries to such stunning successes—and the Japanese before them.

How do you develop a competitive spirit? There are a number of ways.

Keep an ear open for intelligence about your business rivals. You talk to customers all day long; find out what your competition is doing, and, just as important, what they're saying about you. Pass key facts on to your "commanding officer."

Report problems immediately to superiors. If you learn of a customer problem with your product or service that seems serious enough to warrant some rethinking, don't keep this to yourself. Tell the "brass" so something can be done immediately.

Develop a team mentality. Realize that others in your company—administrative people, production people, others in the sales department—are all working toward the same goal you are: success for the firm. Avoid pointless conflicts with coworkers. Share crucial information that will help your company surge ahead. Emphasize positive, optimistic thinking at work.

Set goals and then go all out to attain them. Consider your daily schedule to be a battle plan, then give your every effort over to the goals you establish. Do not allow complacency or acceptance of mediocrity to take root.

There are a number of companies in this country that are already working by the principles outlined above; at the same time, there are many other firms that have institutionalized some work habits that would not pass muster in any real-life fighting unit. It's the companies that have good lines of communication, clearly established goals, and deep commitment to the attainment of results that will flourish in the coming years—and their salespeople will be at the head of the parade.

If you work at such a company, congratulations. If you can work to change your company so that it attains these standards, by all means, do so. If you cannot fight in the army in which you're currently serving, find another army—then give it all you've got.

Good luck!

Not Having a Fallback Position

T. Boone Pickens, a world-class deal-maker during his heyday, contends that it takes as much time to close a big deal as it does to close a little one. I'm not sure that that's true, but I understand the sentiment—as I'm sure you do.

Every sales rep—including a famous sales trainer who shall remain nameless—has gone after what I call the Big Elephant. By that, of course, I mean the Humongous Account, the kind of sale that can define a career.

And who can argue with that? Well, I can. The problem is that invariably reps lay all their eggs in the Big Elephant basket. They become seduced by the possibilities; they start counting—heck they start spending—their commissions. And because they so much want this Big Elephant sale to happen, they concentrate almost exclusively on it and do whatever it takes to close. I think it's a stretch to say they take leave of their senses, but they do seem to lose their sense of hearing.

They hear only what they want to hear and interpret everything positively. They become convinced they are going to land the Elephant. As a result they forget that there are other accounts that need to be served, other prospects that need to be plucked.

Sure, if they land the Elephant everything works out okay. But what if they don't? What if the company changes its mind and goes in a completely different direction? What if there is a sudden spike in the price of gasoline (can you imagine that?), and the company decides to delay introducing the new product?

Here's an example from my own very recent experience. I worked with a large health care operation in Texas. It had 1,400 reps and was in the process of introducing a new product. Based on my meetings with the client, I'd say the odds of my landing this business were 75 to 80 percent in my favor—and I always figure odds conservatively. How was I—or the client, for that matter—to know that the government would issue a regulation preventing companies from selling this type of product? Worse still, they issued the regulation while I was in the air flying to Texas.

My point is that even when sales reps are *this close* to signing a deal, stuff happens.

In the meantime, they've alienated existing clients, done little if any cold calling, and suddenly they discover that their pipeline is empty.

Frankly, even if you do land the account, it is never wise to put all your faith in one large customer. Again, a certain famous sales trainer who shall remain nameless did that. His biggest client was a large international insurance company. He started training its U.S. sales force and over a couple of years began to work with other divisions in different European countries.

Do you really need to hear the rest of this story to know where I'm going? There was a change in personnel at the very top of the company. The new chief executive brought in his people. His people brought in their people. And their people thought the best way to make an impression was to save money by cutting back on training.

Suddenly I—okay, you probably guessed that the nameless sales trainer is me—was on the outside looking in. At first I was told this was just temporary. I was told the contract would be renewed for the next fiscal year. So I figured this was just a temporary setback. Besides, I needed a vacation. But when the next fiscal year came around, the training budget was not restored.

It wasn't like I was forced into bankruptcy or didn't have other business; but, frankly, everything paled in comparison to the big account I lost. I had to make cutbacks in my company and spend a lot of time concentrating on something I should have been doing all along: prospecting, landing new business, building my company.

The irony is that it reinforced a basic axiom I tell my students. In every situation, *you must have a fallback position.* Especially because of the way the international economy has evolved over the last decade, nothing is certain. Today, you can't even count your chickens *after* they've hatched.

I used the example of the Big Account because it so dramatically illustrated my point, but fallback positions are necessary in every phase of sales. I had lunch the other day with a rep who said his one appointment for the day was cancelled. So, with nothing else to do, he was going home after lunch.

91

Clearly, here was a man who had no fallback plan. Also, he probably wasn't aware of his ratios. Sales reps know how many cold calls they have to make to get an appointment and how many appointments it takes to eventually lead to a sale. But there is another "ratio" that is often overlooked—how many appointments are cancelled or postponed.

So what do you do? I say, "Have fallback positions." There is always something that needs to be done: letters, reports, and presentations to write; bills that need to be paid and bills that need to be sent out; and people who need to be contacted and appointments that might be made.

For example, the majority of my clients are based in the New York City area. I keep a list of clients and also potential clients who are based in the area and could do with a follow-up visit. A cancelled appointment gives me a chance to make long overdue calls. "Say, Bill, I'm going to be around the block from you this afternoon. How about a cup of coffee? I have a bunch of new ideas I'd like to talk to you about." (Notice, I didn't say another appointment cancelled.)

Whenever I travel—say to Texas—I always bring extra work with me as well as a list of clients and/or prospects I can call. Once when my appointment was cancelled I found myself with six hours before my return flight. I called a prospect I'd been trying to see for over a year. He had a hole in his schedule and could see me right away. I rented a car, drove in, and we started a dialogue. As of this moment I haven't clinched a sale, but the point is I might—because I had a fallback. And so should you.

Not Asking for the Sale

Part of my preparation when I get a contract to train salespeople at a large corporation is to accompany a few of the company's reps on calls. I speak to the sales managers and corporate executives, of course, but it is going "on rounds" with the sales reps that provides me with the best picture of the company, its product, and the way it is sold. As a result, I'm better able to tailor the class to the students' needs.

But one thing I observe regularly—or at least more regularly than I'd like—is a reluctance on the part of salespeople to ask for the sale. Often they'll say something like, "Suppose I call next Tuesday to get your decision." Or "Do you know when you'll make a decision?"

I suspect there are a number of reasons reps don't ask for the sale. Some may be too polite. They feel that asking just then, face-to-face, might put the prospect on the spot, perhaps embarrassing him or her. Or at least I think that's what most of them tell themselves.

But I believe the main culprit is a lack of confidence in their presentations. They don't believe they've earned the sale and want to put off what they assume (usually correctly) will be a "no."

If this happens to you a lot (or even a little, quite frankly) there are a couple of points that need to be addressed.

First of all, the bottom line is *that you have to ask for the sale no matter how badly you think the presentation went.* I can't make it any plainer than that.

Why do you have to ask for the sale? For one thing, if the answer you receive is "no," what difference does it make if you find out now or two weeks from now? In fact, finding out that the answer is negative now is probably better for you in the long run; it will keep you from worrying about and dwelling on this sale and force you to concentrate on another prospect.

More important, if you get a "no" now, you may be able to find out what went wrong and correct your presentation—*before* a final decision is made—and salvage the business. I make a special point to ask for the sale if I sense something is amiss. Then, if I'm told I didn't make the cut, I say something like: "You know, Bill, I was certain I was on track here. Can you tell me where I went wrong?"

Sometimes I get an answer like, "We just got a new budget and can no longer make as large a commitment to training as we'd anticipated." But often I'll be told a specific area where my proposal went awry. That gives me an opening to try again, to say, "Gee, I should have thought of that myself. Can I rework this and come back to you with a new proposal?"

Getting a "no" gives me an opportunity I never would have had if I waited. Waiting typically means getting a response after a decision is made, when it's too late to do anything but turn tail and walk away with as much grace as you can muster.

But there's another issue here apart from how well the presentation went. Not asking for the sale makes you seem less confident in your ability to make the prospect company perform more efficiently, earn more money, and/or put out a better product.

If you lack confidence, you become tentative—and you make it easy for prospects to say "no" to you. Swagger alone won't necessarily clinch a sale. But a sales rep who demonstrates confidence inspires confidence.

There are a couple of reasons you're not convinced that your product or service is just what the prospect needs. The first is that you haven't done your homework. You haven't spoken to enough people in the company to discover a way to make your product a meaningful part of the prospect company's process. That falls on you. The main focus of the sales process is for you to find a way to make your product seem invaluable to the prospect.

But there's another possible scenario. Perhaps you lack confidence because your product really *is* inferior to others on the market. That happened to me on one of my earliest jobs. I was a good, aggressive salesman, and at first I was able to make a decent enough living, at least for a single young man—even one who lived in Manhattan. But it got to me after a while.

Often the sales I made were because my company was willing to cut prices to the bone, not because the product was the best choice available. Proof that there were very few repeat orders.

I quit after only about six months, determined never to put myself in that kind of situation again. I was young, carefree, and a little idealistic. I know we don't all have those choices. But this is something we should strive for.

Not Getting Enough Information

One of the most important aspects of selling is getting the right information. People sometimes minimize this facet of the process. But, by my count, 90 percent of sales are lost because the rep received incorrect or insufficient information or misinterpreted the info he or she received.

This seems so basic to me that after all these years of teaching I'm still surprised when students come into a classroom believing that information about the product or service they sell is more important than the knowledge they need to accumulate *about the client*. Certainly you have to know your product inside and out. But much more important is how your product can be used by the prospect.

And to understand that, you have to understand the company and how it operates, must discover what the people who use the product do with it, what the person who buys the product wants from suppliers, and how the business functions. And you need to know all that before you can make a recommendation. And then you need to show how using your product or service will help the company do what it does now—better and more profitably.

How do you get the kind of information you need? The first and most obvious way is by asking questions. The common wisdom is that you are supposed to ask "open-ended" questions—that is, questions that cannot be answered with either a "yes" or a "no." That's correct, but it is really much more complicated than that.

Neither you nor the prospect wants to sit there listening to you asking a long list of questions and she answering them. What you want is a conversation that is give and take between the two of you and generates the answers you need.

Not only does that provide information, but engaging the prospect in a conversation involves him in your effort. The give and take of conversation makes the prospect more than an animate source of information; he becomes an active participant in your sales process.

How do you get a conversation going? If you are in sales and do not know how to have a conversation, allow me to respectfully suggest that you may have made a poor career choice. You start a conversation with a prospect the way you start a conversation with a stranger at a party. "Hi, what do you do? How long have you been doing this? What were you doing before?"

But getting enough information from a prospect—say a purchasing manager—alone is only enough if he or she is the only one making the purchasing decision. In that case, there's less need for input from other sources. But if, for example, you sell something that goes through an extensive review process with a final decision made by a committee, it is *imperative* that you use more than one source of information.

It's like the witnesses at an accident. No two people seem to see what happened in the same way. That happens in sales, as well. Some will see your product from the vantage point of cost. Others will see it from an angle of ease of use. That's why I always try to speak to as many as possible to give me a better idea of the complete picture—from all perspectives.

I call it the power of twelve. When I sell to a large corporation I try to touch base with at least a dozen people in all levels of hierarchy. I talk to the company's field sales reps, telemarketers, customer service people, sales managers, sales directs, and VPs. I want to know more about the company than most of the executives do, because the more I know the better able I am to come up with a training solution for what ails them.

That should be your goal as well. If possible, talk to the people in manufacturing to see if there are any problems with the product they currently use, talk to salespeople and see what complaints if any they're getting from customers, talk to sales managers for ideas they may have that might make their product more attractive.

Not only do you learn something from everyone you talk to that can help your cause, every conversation gives you an opportunity to enlist another ally. If someone is unhappy with the cost of widgets from the current supplier and you can show them how much money she'll save, that person becomes an ally. If someone is worried about quality and you can assure him of your product's superiority, well, you have another ally.

In short, you can never have enough information—just as you can never have enough commissions. Coincidence?

NEW MISTAKE #29

Not Knowing When to Stop Talking

Years ago, I saw a poster in my insurance agent's office that I found extremely crude—at first. It said:

Set it up
- *Set it up*
- *Put it down*
- *And shut up*

But the more I thought about it days later, the more I came to recognize the wisdom of those words, especially when it comes to sales. It's impossible to quantify, but I'm convinced that a decent percentage of sales are lost because reps just don't know when to quit talking.

Basically, there are two schools of sales protocol. One says that sales are made and lost in the presentation—that is, in the words brought to the table by the sales rep. The other believes the sales rep's job is not to talk but to listen to what the prospect has to say.

As is always the case, the answer lies somewhere in between. Clearly, as I note in Mistake 28: Not Getting Enough Information, the sales rep needs to speak, and just as obviously the sales rep needs to listen. But that doesn't always happen in the right proportions.

More often than not, the problem is associated with the sales rep's ego. We've all met the rep who thinks he knows it all—and isn't shy about informing everyone around him about how smart he is. Let's assume for a minute that you are an expert in your product. You know how it is manufactured. You know how it can be used. You know how it should be sold.

What happens if someone comes in and tells you everything you know is completely false, that he knows the real truth and you ought to be grateful that he is willing to share it with you? What do you think you'd tell him? Do the words "shut up" come to mind?

Let's say someone comes in and spends the preponderance of time at the meeting talking about her exploits—how many widgets she's sold, how many companies she works with, all the places her widgets are used—without a word about how you might use them. What might your reaction be? Do the words "shut up" come to mind?

Or how about a sales rep who does ask appropriate questions but doesn't bother to listen to your answers. As a result, his proposal is wildly off base. What might your reaction be? Do the words "shut up" come to mind?

It's not like I don't occasionally feel the urge to blabber; we all do. But the guidepost I use is to ask myself how I would feel if I were on the receiving end of this conversation. Would I want me to stop? Would I feel enough had been said?

I also have a simple "know-when-to-stop-talking" plan. Before I go into a meeting I note what I want to accomplish. It may be just to get some questions answered. It may be to see if I can get an okay to meet additional folks at the company. It may be to get "righted"—that is to see if the information I've received to date—and my interpretation of it—is accurate. Once I achieve my goal (and set up the next step), I get out of there as quickly as I can politely do so.

Ben Franklin famously said, "Fish and visitors smell in three days." Steve Schiffman says, "Nothing can stink up a deal faster than a sales rep who doesn't know when to stop talking."

The shut up rule is even more important when you present. You offer your proposal, repeat points of emphasis, and then keep quiet. You might ask if there are any questions, any points that need clarification, or even ask for an order.

But don't keep repeating yourself. Very few things are worse than a salesperson droning on and on, repeating points as though the prospects were idiots and didn't get the point the first four times he brought them up.

Silence can be an important weapon in your arsenal. It's okay to let the prospect fill the quietude.

The bottom line is if your message is appropriate and properly delivered, the prospect will get it. If it's not, then no matter how much you talk, you won't be able to overcome that blunder.

And on the subject of blunders, please allow me to recount a sadly true story. I'd clinched a sale (in my mind, anyway), said goodbye, and on the way out asked if I could use the phone. The prospect said yes and while I was dialing picked up a book and asked me what I thought of it.

I reacted negatively, only to discover he wrote one of the book's sections. When I finished the call, the prospect said, "We may have to rethink this." I lost the sale. If only I had followed my own advice and just got out of there without saying another word . . .

Remember to do as I say, not as I do.

NEW MISTAKE #30

Taking a Leisurely Sales Approach

With apologies to Albert Einstein, let me point out that the only resource that salespeople can't expand is time.

But as Einstein himself might have said, everything is relative. For some reps, time is not an issue. Using a slightly off-beat example, a door-to-door salesperson knocks on a door, talks about his vacuum cleaner, and gets a yes or no. Reaction is instantaneous and time doesn't play a role in whether or not he makes a sale.

But for most of us, selling is a time-consuming process, and the bottom line is that the longer the process takes, the less likely that you'll actually clinch a sale. The reason is that you are more susceptible to outside influences. The door-to-door person gets a yes or no and it's a done deal—or it isn't. There's no two ways about it.

But over the course of a lengthy negotiation, you're faced with the possibility of a lot of outside factors negatively impacting your sale. Consider the sales rep for Boeing. I'm sure that the process for each sale she makes takes a couple of years. For the sake of argument let us assume that the rep—after two year's hard work—is ready to sign a deal with Air France. But then the value of the franc sinks against the dollar and the airline has to call the deal off. Or, as we've seen recently, the price of fuel jumps precipitously, and the airline has to call the deal off.

There are probably dozens of other factors that can similarly affect a sale: the company is bought out or merges, your contact leaves or is promoted to an unrelated job, the economy takes a downturn, the company goes in a different direction. You get the point—but not the sale.

While this primarily affects reps with long sales cycles, it can hurt anyone in sales. You can be on the verge of signing a contract one day and find that a corporate upheaval caught everyone by surprise and changed everything overnight.

So what to do? Obviously, you don't waste any time. Some of us—and I've occasionally been guilty of this myself—count our chickens and commissions before they hatch. So we ease up. We assume we're going to get the deal, so there's no need to pressure the prospective client. Besides, now that we have this one wrapped up, we can devote more energy to another prospect.

Again with apologies to Einstein, *dawdling equals many missed contract closings*—or, as I call it, D = MC^2.

What to do? Every prospect is different. Every prospect-sales rep relationship is different. But within the confines of your ties to the prospect, the idea is to push for prompt follow-ups. If you want a second meeting tell him you can get him that info by tomorrow afternoon. Can you see him at three?

If you're ready to make a formal proposal, schedule an appointment sooner rather than later—especially if you think you have the goods to present. If you've gotten far enough along in the sales process where the prospect company seems genuinely interested, take advantage of it—especially when a delay can cool things off.

If at all possible, try to create a time frame with your prospect early on. Right at the start, at a second or third meeting, you can ask, "If things work out as I think they will, when would you need deliveries to start?"

You have to have a sense of urgency, and you should imbue your prospects with it as well. How do you do that? Let me begin by telling you how not to do it. A salesman recently came into my office and told me; if I purchased his product he would win a trip to Hawaii, I held his trip and happiness in my hands. You know what? I didn't care. That was a fake sense of urgency, and I resented the fact that he tried to pressure me with something that would benefit him. The nerve!

A better example concerns a new phone system I just ordered for my office from Verizon. The saleswoman told me that in order to meet my schedule—that is, to get the phones up and operating when I needed them—I'd actually have to sign that very day and set up my installation appointments. Otherwise she couldn't guarantee that the job would get done in time. Of course I signed up right away.

Another example: we worked with a large company that was about to introduce a significant new piece of commercial software, a large leap forward from what it currently offered. The executives I was dealing with were hemming and hawing: should they do it, do they have to do it now, maybe things would work out by themselves.

All that changed when I told them they were facing two problems: not only did they have to train their sales force to sell the software, they had to train the salespeople how to use the program so they could demonstrate its benefits to potential customers. If they were going to do that in time for the new product rollout, they'd have to do it now. And they did.

There are other ways to create a sense of urgency: limited time offers, seasonality (to get these toys in time for Christmas . . .), warnings of an upcoming price increase.

But no matter what you do or how you do it, the onus is on you to keep the process going.

Quick Reference Summary

MISTAKE #1
Not Being Obsessed
Maintain a commitment to results every single moment you are at work; utilize tools and implement ideas quickly.

MISTAKE #2
Not Listening to the Prospect
Never interrupt. Get key facts, isolate problems, and send the right message, both verbally and nonverbally: "I am here to help you."

MISTAKE #3
Not Empathizing with the Prospect
Try to see the other person's perspective; remember that you are not going to be thought of as the most important item on the day's agenda. Develop respect for the prospect's time.

MISTAKE #4
Seeing the Prospect as an Adversary
Strive to get the prospect to work with you; do not approach the sale from a confrontational mindset.

MISTAKE #5
Getting Distracted
Concentrate throughout your meeting; do not become disoriented by confusing or negative remarks from the prospect.

MISTAKE #6
Not Taking Notes
Establish control and reinforce the prospect's desire to offer information by taking down key facts on a note pad.

MISTAKE #7
Failing to Follow Up
Send professional-looking thank-you notes at key points in the sales cycle.

MISTAKE #8
Not Keeping in Contact with Past Clients
Remember that someone who decides to use your product or service, then falls out of your current customer base, may still be a highly qualified lead.

MISTAKE #9
Not Planning the Day Efficiently
Commit to a daily schedule and measure your actual performance against it.

MISTAKE #10
Not Looking Your Best
Put forward a sharp, well-groomed, professional image when dealing with prospects.

MISTAKE #11
Not Keeping Sales Tools Organized
Make sure your briefcase, sample cases, and other materials are neatly organized and reinforce your overall professional image.

MISTAKE #12
Not Taking the Prospect's Point of View
Isolate product benefits and highlight these for the prospect.

MISTAKE #13
Not Taking Pride in Your Work
Stand behind your product and your company with pride; talk frequently with others about what you do for a living.

MISTAKE #14
Trying to Convince, Rather Than Convey
Demonstrate in a compelling way how your product or service can address relevant concerns. Do not apply "high pressure" sales tactics that ignore the needs of the prospect.

MISTAKE #15
Underestimating the Prospect's Intelligence
Strive to act as a conveyor of information; work with the prospect to identify problems and find workable solutions.

MISTAKE #16
Not Keeping Up to Date
Do not assume that once a sale has closed you need no longer attempt to learn about the problems of the customer. Develop contacts and monitor relevant publications to detect key trends in a given industry.

MISTAKE #17
Rushing the Sale
Let the sales cycle progress at the pace that's most appropriate for the prospect.

MISTAKE #18
Not Using People Proof
Build credibility by highlighting past successes with other customers.

MISTAKE #19
Humbling Yourself
Operate from the assumption that you bring to the table a specific set of skills and a level of product knowledge that the other person can benefit from. Work with the prospect as a partner, not a supplicant.

MISTAKE #20
Being Fooled by "Sure Things"
Do not become distracted with sales on the horizon; this reduces your effectiveness in developing your customer base today.

MISTAKE #21
Taking Rejection Personally
Try to develop resilience and self-assurance when confronting rejection; remember that hearing a "no" answer is the only way to get to a "yes" answer.

MISTAKE #22
Not Assuming Responsibility
When faced with a "no" answer, consider asking the prospect where you have gone wrong, or what mistakes you have made in the presentation.

MISTAKE #23
Underestimating the Importance of Prospecting
Develop good prospecting skills, and work daily to find new customers.

MISTAKE #24
Focusing on Negatives
Approach obstacles from a positive frame of mind; avoid negative habits such as complaining and gossiping.

MISTAKE #25
Not Showing Competitive Spirit
Establish strong "battlefield strategies" that will help your "army" attain its objectives.

NEW MISTAKE #26
Not Having a Fallback Position
Keep a plan in your pocket for when something goes wrong.

NEW MISTAKE #27
Not Asking for the Sale
Have confidence in your presentation and product.

NEW MISTAKE #28
Not Getting Enough Information
Use your conversational skills to get to know the client—what he wants, what he needs, and how you can help.

NEW MISTAKE #29
Not Knowing When to Stop Talking
Know what you want to accomplish, talk just enough to meet your goal, and then shut up.

NEW MISTAKE #30
Taking a Leisurely Sales Approach
If you create a time frame with a sense of urgency built into it, your customers will sense it too.

About the Author

Stephan Schiffman has trained over 250,000 salespeople at firms such as AT&T Information Systems, Chemical Bank, Manufacturers Hanover Trust, Motorola, and U.S. Healthcare. Mr. Schiffman, president of DEI Management Group, is the author of *Cold Calling Techniques (That Really Work!)*, *The 25 Most Common Sales Habits of Highly Successful Salespeople*, and a number of other popular books on sales.

Do you have questions, comments, or suggestions regarding this book? Please share them with me! Write to me at this address: *sschiffman@steveschiffman.com*.